—◦◦⊰{ POEMS AFTER MARTIAL }⊱◦◦—

POEMS AFTER

MARTIAL

BY

Philip Murray

WESLEYAN UNIVERSITY PRESS

Middletown, Connecticut

Library of Congress Catalog Card Number: 67–24109

Manufactured in the United States of America

FIRST EDITION

This book is dedicated to
Richard Ringheim

Contents

—⸰•❧{ POEMS AFTER MARTIAL }❧•⸰—

The Art of Creative Translation:
or
Critics, Disarm

My knowledge of Latin, although derived from good sources, Christian Brothers and Jesuit Fathers, is imperfect. But then, so is yours. And this is first of all a book of poems. The author is more of a poet than a scholar.

This is a book of creative translations that aspires to demonstrate without fustian footnotes and humourless explanations that Marcus Valerius Martialis, the great epigrammatist of first-century Rome, is still the funniest poet alive.

Listen to this:

BOOK X:xv
Dotatae uxori cor harundine fixit acuta,
sed dum ludit, Aper. ludere novit Aper.

There is a strong presumption that only a handful of classical scholars like William Arrowsmith and Gilbert Highet are laughing. But if your Latin were not so rusty, or so nonexistent, you would be laughing too. A word-for-word translation of these lines will be slightly amusing, but the spontaneous force of the epigram is completely lost. Here is the Loeb Classical Library prose version by Walter C. A. Ker:

His well-dowered wife's heart Aper transfixed with a sharp arrow, but it was in sport. Aper is a clever sportsman.

Here is James Elphinston's eighteenth-century version:

With a sly shaft he shot his dowried wife.
Arch Aper knows the game, and plays for life.

This is not Elphinston at his worst by any means, but it is well to keep in mind that Dr. Johnson growled amiably at Elphinston's translations. "He did not ask my advice, and I did not force it upon him to make him angry."

Doubtless the doctor wanted something more like this version of Martial XI:lxvii, which headed *The Rambler*, No. 198:

A Hinted Wish

You told me, Maro, whilst you live
You'd not a single penny give,
But that, whene'er you chanct to die,
You'd leave a handsome legacy:
You must be mad beyond redress,
If my next wish you cannot guess!

This is not by Johnson, although it has been on occasion erroneously attributed to him. It is the work of Rev. Francis Lewis of Chiswick, of whom Boswell says nothing is known except that he "lived in London and hung loose upon society."

But Johnson was fond of Martial, and as the author of an early and lost "Latin Verses on a Glow-Worm"—one of his "first essays"—he had a right to growl. Elphinston's own brother-in-law offered him £50 to desist. But he did not. Robert Burns cried "Murther" even on his fellow Scot.

But let's return to Martial, Book X:xv. Here is a version by Paul Nixon from his book of Martial translations, *A Roman Wit* (1911):

Play's the Thing

Aper pierced his wife's heart with an arrow
While playing, friends say.
The wife was exceedingly wealthy:
He knows how to play.

This is what I make of it:

ARCHERY ACCIDENT: APER'S WIFE TRANSFIXED

When a sportsman weds an heiress,
His aim is apt to get careless.

4

Take another example—a distich much more familiar:

BOOK V:xliii

Thais habet nigros, niveos Laecania dentes.
    quae ratio est? emptos haec habet, illa suos.

R. Fletcher (1656)—not Beaumont's Fletcher—has this translation:

Thais her teeth are black and nought,
    Lecania's white are grown:
But what's the reason? these are bought,
    The other wears her own.

The following is by William Hay, M.P. for Seaford (1755):

Nell's teeth are white, but Betty's teeth are brown;
Hemmet's Nell's are; but Betty's are her own.

In 1950 the magazine *Imagi* (Vol. 5, no. 2) printed this version by Ezra Pound:

Thais has black teeth, Laecania's are white   because
    she bought 'em last night.

My version will illustrate my method. The title and the parody of a certain popular lyricist are intended to augment the joke.

Getting to Know Laecania
SUD denly she's BRIGHT and BREEZ y
Be CAUSE of ALL THE
BEAU ti ful AND NEW
Denture.

But the popular conception of Martial as a cynical and bawdy wit who wrote mostly two-liners has to be modified considerably. He has at least one "epigram" of fifty-one lines, and his range is far wider than is generally recognized. He is at times touching, tender, shrewd, sophisticated, elegiac, or pastoral, depending on the particular poem. Some of his best poems are not epigrams at all, as he himself was well aware, even though he published them

5

all under such a title.

More than three-fourths of Martial's fifteen hundred poems are written in elegiacs—a distich or series of distichs made up of one hexameter line followed by a pentameter line—a meter he took over from Catullus. Perhaps Coleridge's mnemonic will help the reader with the Latin rhythm of such lines.

> In the hexameter rises the fountain's silvery column;
> In the pentameter, aye, falling in melody back.

Elegiacs, as you see, do not go very gracefully into English poetry, and especially not if one is joking. It is almost always a fatal error to attempt English poems of any kind in the original Latin meters. The temptation is always present, but I trust it is one of the virtues of my little book that I have staunchly resisted it.

Let me give you one example of the sort of embalmed flamingo style in original Latin meters that I have sedulously spared my readers. This is James Cranstoun's version of Martial's lovely poem in elegiacs, Book III:lxv, taken from the Random House Modern Library Latin Poets volume (No. 217)—a volume almost uniformly old guard, of which this is a prime specimen. The volume dates from 1949, and no date is given for the translation.

To Diadumenus
Sweet as perfume of an apple bit by tooth of tender maiden,
　　Or as zephyr from Corycian saffron-glade—
Sweet as branches of the vine with snow-white virgin
　　　　blossoms laden,
　　Or as plains when sheep have newly cropped the
　　　　blade—

Sweet as myrtle, or as Arab that has come from reaping
　　　　spices,
　　Or as amber warmed by friction's heating power—
Sweet as from Assyrian incense is the pale-blue flame that
　　　　rises,
　　Or as delvèd soil bedewed by summer shower—

Sweet as breathes the circling garland round the nard-
    anointed tresses,
  Is thy kiss, cold Diadumenus! to me:
Oh, would that thou wouldst freely shower on me thy fond
    caresses,
  All those sweets and more than all I'd find in thee!

I need not give you my translation here. It has to be better.

In the following poem Martial's elegiacs are put to exact elegiac use in one of his tenderest poems:

BOOK V:xxxiv

Hanc tibi, Fronto pater, genetrix Flaccilla, puellam
  oscula commendo deliciasque meas,
parvola ne nigras horrescat Erotion umbras
  oraque Tartarei prodigiosa canis.
inpletura fuit sextae modo frigora brumae,
  vixisset totidem ni minus illa dies.
inter tam veteres ludat lasciva patronos
  et nomen blaeso garriat ore meum.
mollia non rigidus caespes tegat ossa nec illi,
  terra, gravis fueris: non fuit illa tibi.

Is it generally known that Robert Louis Stevenson planned a volume of Martial translation (from a French crib) in 1884? He completed about sixteen poems, but the book was never finished. It is a pity, for his versions are as good as any we have to date and are well worth a reader's curiosity. Here is his translation of "Hanc tibi, Fronto . . ."

Here Lies Erotion

Mother and sire, to you do I commend
Tiny Erotion, who must now descend,
A child, among the shadows, and appear
Before hell's bandog and hell's gondolier.
Of six hoar winters she had felt the cold,
But lacked six days of being six years old.
Now she must come, all playful, to that place

Where the great ancients sit with reverend face;
Now lisping, as she used, of whence she came.
Perchance she names and stumbles at my name.
O'er these so fragile bones, let there be laid
A plaything for a turf, and for that maid
That ran so lightly footed in her mirth
Upon thy breast—lie lightly mother earth!

In 1963 Rolfe Humphries published his hexameter version of this poem in his book of Martial translations from Indiana University Press:

BOOK V:xxxiv

To you, Fronto, my father, and mother Flaccilla, I tender
This little servant-maid, joy and delight of my heart.
Don't let her shiver and shake in the horrible blackness of
    Hades,
Don't let her be afraid of the Hell-hound's horrible jaws.
She had arrived, almost, at one more of her birthdays in
    winter,
Almost six years old, missing by only six days.
Now let her romp as she will in the sight of her aged
    protectors,
Let her lisping voice utter the sound of my name;
Let the turf above her delicate bones lie gently;
Rest on her lightly, O earth; she was not heavy on thee.

The reader will find my version in the pages of this book.

But if one may take an absolute view of Martial in English, the laurel may still go to the Elizabethans, some of them anonymous, who in spite of their limitations (they made Martial an Elizabethan courtier) and their reservations (William Webbe in an essay of 1586 refers to "Martiall, a most dissolute wryter," and in 1593, Gabriel Harvey, he who tried to dissuade Spenser from writing "The Faerie Queene," speaks of "The swines-meate of Martial") have done Martial the fullest justice to date.

Here is a small sampling of Elizabethan Martial. The first

two are by Sir John Harrington, Queen Elizabeth's godson and her favorite court poet.

From Book II:xx:

Of Don Pedro and His Poetry

Sir, I shall tell you newes, except you know it,
Our noble friend Don Pedro is a Poet.
His verses all abroad are read and showne,
And he himself doth sweare they are his owne.
His owne? tis true, for he for them hath paid
Two crownes a Sonnet, as I heard it said.
So Ellen hath faire teeth, that in her purse
She keepes all night, and yet sleepes ne'er the worse.
So widdow Lesbia, with her painted hide,
Seem'd, for the time, to make a handsome bride.
    If Pedro be for this a Poet cald,
    So you may call one hairie that is bald.

And from the Book VI:xii:

    The golden hair that Galla wears
        Is hers: who would have thought it?
    She swears 'tis hers, and true she swears,
        For I know where she bought it.

Ben Jonson has these lines to Tucca (Book XII:xciv):

I cannot for the stage a drama lay,
Tragic or comic, but thou writ'st a play.
I learn thee there, and, giving way, intend
An epic poem; thou hast the same end.
I modestly quit that, and think to write
Next morn an ode; thou mak'st a song ere night.
I pass to elegies; thou meet'st me there;
To satires, and thou dost pursue me. Where,
Where shall I scape thee? In an epigram?
Oh! thou cri'st out, that is my proper game.

This is the justly famous version of Book X:xlvii by Henry

Howard, the Earl of Surrey:

The Means to Attain Happy Life
Martial, the things that do attain
    The happy life be these, I find:
The riches left, not got with pain;
    The fruitful ground, the quiet mind.
The equal friend, no grudge, no strife,
    No charge of rule nor governance;
Without disease, the healthful life;
    The household of continuance.
The mean diet, no delicate fare;
    True wisdom joined with simpleness;
The night discharged of all care,
    Where wine the wit may not oppress.
The faithful wife, without debate;
    Such sleeps as may beguile the night.
Contented with thine own estate,
    Ne wish for death, ne fear his might.

And here is our previously embalmed flamingo in a more mellifluous guise; an anonymous version from an old sixteenth-century manuscript:

BOOK III:lxv
As apples smell bitt by a young girle's tooth,
Or winde past o'er a field of saffron doth;
As flowr'y vines when their first budds forth peepe,
Or fragrant grass new cropt by tender sheepe;
As myrtle or the Arabian mowers scent;
Chaft gums, or fumes which spices burnt present:
As furrows gently sprinkled with heat showers,
As locks oyled with nard and crown'd with flowers:
So smell thy half-lipp'd kisses, cruell fayre;
If freely giv'n how sweeter much they were!

Nevertheless, Martial is a poet for *our* time. There is fortunately no need to make Martial into a modern poet. He *is* a modern poet, and much closer to us than to the Elizabethans, though the reasons for this are not always complimentary to our age.

Martial is a great satirist, but because he wrote "epigrams" he is frequently excluded from the company of other satirists, and there are many prominent books on satire that do not even mention his name. The classicists seem to have agreed tacitly that while Martial is frequently satiric in content, his form is primarily epigrammatic, and that is a horse of another color.

Most often, Martial sees vice as folly, and folly makes him laugh. Some of the laughter (about one-fourth of his entire work) is outrageously obscene even by today's lax standards. These poems I have mercifully left alone; but there are some raucous poems included in this book. It is to be hoped I have not overstepped the bounds of good taste.

There may be a live rabbit or two here, but there are no stuffed owls and no limericks. These poems are not intended to be imitations. They are meant to be the essence of Martial presented in English, based with reasonable aesthetic latitude on their Latin source. To my mind, every translator is an adapter in some sense. English cannot be Latin, nor should it try to be. A good translation must be a good poem.

The translator has brought more than twenty years of his own poems to bear on this project. It is to be hoped that many readers will be encouraged by these efforts to consult the original Latin texts in order to judge for themselves the merits of the present endeavor and, what is more important, to become better acquainted with Martial. My book means to testify on behalf of one such salutary confrontation.

PHILIP MURRAY

New York City
July, 1967

Martial

Marcus Valerius Martialis was born in Bilbilis, Spain, about 40 A.D., and died there about 104 A.D. He spent most of his mature years in Rome.

The Reason

I don't send you *my* work.
You might send me *your* work.

Brevity

What's the good of brevity
If it makes a book?

To One Reader

You read my book as if it were yours;
The way you read it, I wish it were.

Thanks

Thanks for the holiday presents.
Thanks for the six three-leaved tablets;
Thanks for the seven toothpicks;
Thanks for the sponge, the napkin and cup;
Thanks for the small figs and the dried prunes;
All the junk you didn't want
Carried to me in full procession
By your bevy of Syrian slaves.
One small boy might have brought
Five pounds of silver plate.

A Dinner Party

Stella, Nepos, Canius, Cerialis, Flaccus,
They're all coming; but we're only six tonight
And the couch holds seven. Won't you join us, Lupus?
I'm calling it a modest dinner party;
You know it's just another beggars' levee.

My housekeeper will scare up some garden fare,
The usual roughage, mallows and leek, lettuce and rocket;
And I've got a skinny lizard-fish to serve
Which can be smothered in sliced eggs and mint.
The others will think it's perch if you keep quiet.

For the main course, there's a slightly damaged kid
Snatched from the jaws of a wolf, but edible,
Meat-balls so tender you won't need your knife,
Beans and sprouts. And I will add to these
A chicken and ham left from my last dinner.

When you're full, I'll pass around the apples,
New wine without lees, lots of good jokes, all harmless.
You can argue charioteers, but no real disputes;
My dinners never lead to lawsuits.
Do come, and bring some cheese or fruit.

Advice to Fabianus

Fabianus, good man, true in heart and tongue,
Why have you come to Rome?
Unless you want to be a pander,
Or a pretty boy, or an informer,
Or a seducer of your friend's wife,
Or a lecher after old women's fortunes,
Or a sycophant about the palace,
Fabianus, go home.

Lines to a Slow Reader

"Publish, publish," you cried.
After two pages, you're tired
And turn to the end with a frown,
Over poems you copied down
In manuscript, and passed around
At the theatre and after dinner.
God knows my book is thinner
Than a one-sided pancake.
Are you going to take six months
To read all of it once?
How lazy can a dilettante be?
Does any sensible traveller
Change horses each half-mile?
Severus, read my book promptly,
And don't forget to smile.

At Erotion's Grave

Father, mother, blessed shadows prepare
To greet a tender child, my precious friend,
Erotion, six days shy of winters six.
She fears the dark. And then if Cerberus
Should bark, what little girl is not afraid?
Her games have always been more brief than brave.
She has a charming lisp that sometimes stumbles
Over my name. Cherish these halting sounds.
Earth, bear softly, on her delicate bones
As light as footsteps, once, above hard ground.

The Point

The cuckold finally caught the culprit,
Boxed his ears and broke his jaw.
But hasn't he missed the point?

Poet of Your Choice

Don't send _____ _____ any of my work.
He can read, but he's a jerk.

To a Cuckold

Your wife's lover's nose, stuffed, on the mantel;
You never learned to take life by the handle.

To a Stoic

Nobody praises death
Like you, poor stoic,
In your short rough toga,
With your cold hearth,
Your threadbare rug,
Lumpy bed full of bugs,
Broken jugs, black bread,
And just the dregs of wine.

I don't admire a mind
So easily resigned.

If you had a cozy couch
With plush pillows,
And a handsome lad
Who turned all heads
To toss your salad,
Then you'd be glad
To hold fast;
Nestor, he died young!

But strong men last,
Even when they're wretched.

The Menu

You ask me to dinner; I gladly come.
You have oysters; I have seashells.
You get mushrooms; I get swine-fungus.
You have perch; I get brill.
You eat a plump golden turtle-dove;
I'm served a blackbird that died in its cage.
Needless to say, I won't come again;
That's a menu for Janus, not for friends.

In Stock

Whenever we meet, Lupercus, you say,
"I mean to read your book of epigrams;
May I send my boy to fetch it one day?"
There is no need for such a trip.
It's a long way to Pear Tree Street
And I live three high flights up.
Your local bookseller is nearer. I'm in stock.
There's a shop across from Caesar's Forum
With an ad on the doorpost listing me,
And if you merely ask for poetry,
The gentleman will pull out my little volume
With its appropriately purple trimmings.
I suspect you think I'm not worth the price.
You're not bright, Lupercus; but you're wise.

To a Sick Friend

Ten times a year or more, you take to your bed.
All those get-well gifts, all that fuss . . .
It doesn't hurt you, it hurts us.
Do your friends a favor. Drop dead.

The Widower's Wine

Whenever I come to dine,
You bring out the celebrated wine
Which rumour has it
Made you a widower several times.
I don't believe a word of it,
But when you serve me—
I am never thirsty.

The Old Man's Case

I am not in court for any assault
Or poisoning, or any such thing.
I am here about three she-goats;
I can prove my neighbor stole them.
Now I know these walls mostly ring
With rhetoric about the Punic Wars,
Perjuries and plots. Still I hope
You will soon get to my three she-goats.

A Farm?

This is a farm, Lupus?
My window is wider.
Diana's grove is a single rue plant?
It could be eaten by one glutted ant.
There isn't space for an uncurled snake,
A cucumber couldn't lie straight.

The garden might feed a caterpillar,
But a gnat could consume that willow.
Who wants a mole for a ploughman?
How could figs split or mushrooms expand?
A mouse ravages the borders
With wild barbarian disorders.

There isn't room by half
For Priapus and his mighty staff.
My harvest fits in a snail shell,
My wine is stored in a nutshell,
Lupus, thanks for the farm, but hell,
I'm staying in town.

Comme il est

Aemilianus, if among millionaires,
You are only a Poverty Czar,
Don't grumble, *mon semblable, mon frère;*
That's the way Fortuna's cookies crumble.

Praise for Phidias

These fish were carved by Phidias;
Add water and they will swim.

On the Death of the Barber Boy

Here lies the little barber boy of Pear Tree Street,
Pantagathus, whose fingers were so deft, so fleet
In cutting hair and trimming beards, far beyond
His callow years, he was the master of his art.
Clumsy Death has broken his master's heart and mine
Over this quick, unlucky lad; Earth, be kind.

Dining at Milo's

If you're dining at Milo's,
I hope you like squash.
He cuts each into a thousand pieces
As if it were the sons of Thyestes
And he were Atreus.
At once, squash salad,
And after, squash soup,
And then squash mincemeat,
Then lentils and beans
(Squash in disguise),
Mushrooms and black pudding
(More squash in disguise),
And then for dessert,
Squash cakes and squash candy
Wrapped in rue leaves for variety.
He's proud of his amenities,
And you must concede
They're lavish penny dinners, indeed.

Elementary

Do the children crowd around your desk?
That's the test. It isn't in the text,
But school should be like play.
Put down those straps and paddles;
Lessons aren't battles.
Boys learn most in summer anyway.

Shopping

Mamurra dawdled all day in the market place.
He ogled every slave in sight, and even all
Those choicer subjects cached behind curtains,
Conserved for opulent fastidious stalls.
His eyes, surfeited with flesh, turned next
To tables with ivory legs and circular tops;
He spared no trouble to see the entire stock;
Items hung high in the rafters, he had brought down;
Those in deep shadows were dragged into the light.
He compared and compared, before deciding to wait.

Four times he measured a tortoise-shell couch
For six, but sighed it was too small for his needs.
He sniffed bronzes; they were not Corinthian.
He scrutinized crystal vases; each had some blemish.
The porcelain plates he had put aside, he ordered replaced,
While he studied an antique tankard embossed with gems.
He weighed some pearls, pronounced a ruby fake,
And inquired the price of one large jasperlike stone;
Then, as he was weary and it was getting late,
He purchased two crude clay cups and scampered home.

Man to Man

Who rocked me in my cradle? You did.
Who taught me how to toddle? You did.
Who dragged me out of wells and ditches?
Who scrubbed my face and changed my britches?
Who held my hand when the brown cow mooed?
You did. You did.
BUT I have grown up.
And up, and up.
I have a beard, I drink, I rut.
You can't forbid it; why not admit it?
Your sermons, scoldings, whippings, must cease.
A man's entitled to a little peace.
I AM a man; twice I have proved it.
What's more—both times your mistress loved it.

My Juvenilia

If you want to see the doggerel
Of my youth, my wretched juvenilia
Which I no longer recognize
And have since cast aside,
(And if you have leisure to waste
And wish to punish your good taste)
You can read several poems
Every week in *The New Roman**
Where trifles in that old style
Still flourish like fake flowers.

*The New Roman was an ancient weekly of advertising, remembered mostly for its jokes. Edited in its high period mainly by Rossius, Mossius, and Cauda Linea. Occasional reviews by Nil Admirari.

Where Have I Heard That Name?

Someone named Cinna writes verses against me.
Who in the empire can he possibly be?
Cinna Gallia, Cinna Roma? Cinna Rama?
Cinna Bad the Sailor? Cinna Qua Non?
The Original Cinna, or one of the deadly Seven?

Doctor Spartacus: Eye Specialist

"If I'm not in my Office,
Dial CIrcus 2-0006."

Gifts

Sabellus is rich;
What holiday gifts!
He's bragging up and down
There's no luckier lawyer in town.
And the cause of all this windy pride
Is a half-peck of crushed beans,
Three half-pounds of frankincense and pepper,
A flagon of black must and a string of sausages,
One jar of fig jelly, some snails and a cheese;
Not to mention a small box of large olives,
A set of seven clay cups from Spain, *embossed,*
And a handkerchief with broad vulgar stripes,
The kind bald Senators blow their distinguished noses in.
Lucky, lucky him!

Advice to Scaevola

"Ye gods," you cried, "If I had the money,
How lavishly I should live."
The gods, who enjoy being funny,
Granted your wish. You're rich.
Yet your clothes are coarse; your manners, worse.
Your shoes are patched; your socks don't match;
You need a comb, you constantly scratch;
You live in rooms abandoned by rats.
A stingy dinner for six serves eleven;
Out of ten large olives, you hoard seven.
That tepid brine you call pea soup
Costs as little as your penny love-whoops.
You drink nothing but the worst red wine,
Neatest when returned to the jar as urine.
As a wealthy man you're a foolish fraud,
The butt of bored and playful gods.
If you're only going to live like a beggar,
Give me the money. I'll show them better.

Odious Comparisons

A swamp in summer, a putrid pond,
A rutting goat, a soured wine,
Sulphur springs, busy latrines;
These are a few of the foulest things;
Rancid oils, a nest of vipers,
The loincloth of a scabrous leper,
A garlic breath, a mouldy cheese;
When I consider all of these,
I tell myself—it's true, but sad—
Bassa, you don't smell so bad.

One Question

Vacerra, since you really are such a prodigiously and
phenomenally calculating son of a bitch,
Why aren't you rich?

A Sad Case

A wig, you can buy.
Teeth, you can buy.
But Laelia, an eye?

Homage to Erotion

Here, among quickening shades, Erotion rests
Whom winter storms have borne to earth at five
Green years. I beg you, Sir, lord of this field
When I depart, to pay her yearly homage.
So may the gods protect your hearth
And spare you early tears, except upon this stone.

A Certain Dinner for Thirty

A dinner for thirty—
And what was the fare?
There were no grapes,
There were no honey apples,
There were no pears,
There were no pomegranates,
There were no olives,
There were no cheeses,
There was only this boar,
And a tiny one, too,
That could have been killed
By an unarmed dwarf.
And after, we sat around
Gazing at nothing, intently.

The Villa of Julius Martialis

The few fields of my good friend Julius
Are sweeter than the gardens of Hesperides.
Orchard, vineyard, wide secluded groves,
Lie flat on top of long Janiculum,
With broad backs bent, swelling to gentle hills.
When fog drifts down concealing crooked valleys,
His fields alone rise free into the clear sky,
Shining unclouded in their own special light.
The graceful rooftops of this lofty villa
Lift it to the level of brilliant stars.

From this side you may see the seven hills
And take the measurement of Rome completely,
The Alban Hills, the Tusculan Hills, all
The cool retreats that cluster near a city.
From that side you may see carriages
On the Flaminian or the Salarian Way,
But you will not hear the sound of carriage wheels,
And though the Milvian Bridge is near,
Neither bosun's call, nor bargeman's shout
On the swift Tiber, will interrupt your dreams.

This country place—or should I say this town house?—
Its owner commends to you so generously
And with such genial hospitality,
That you will think you have a claim upon it
Like another Hercules, or a new Ulysses
Accepting kindness on some hazardous journey.

You to whom all this is small nowadays
May dig up your many acres with a hundred hoes.
I prefer the few fields of my good friend Julius.
I could be quite contented with those.

The Only Book

I write too many poems, I know.
It's the rare wine that pleases,
The earliest spring apples, snowy roses.
Even mistresses learn how to say no;
A door always open is not often closed.
A good couplet will outlast a bad epic.
Since these things are so, next time
You read a book of mine, pretend
It's my only book and you will find
One briefer and better than I designed.

A Too Sedulous Ape

I began an epic on the brothers Gracchi;
You began your epic "The Brothers Gracchi."
So I undertook a tragedy, "Sulla's Revenge";
So you undertook your tragedy, "The Revenge of Sulla."
I composed a Calabrian songbook;
You composed your "Songs of Old Calabria."
I tried satire; you tried satire.
Then I turned to elegy, "Cleopatra's Farewell."
Then you turned to elegy, "An Aspic's Trail."
Now, as a last resort, I have taken up epigrams;
Tucca, if, as a last retort, you take up epigrams,
WHAM!

A Switch

It's Hallowe'en.
Charisianus gets all dressed up
Like a human being.

Accomplished?

Phyllis plays late Beethoven sonatas
With one hand.
Fan TAS tic? One-handed.

Caveat Lector

So far Mona, so far Lisa, my book has been pleasing
To ingénues and matrons, all innocence and prudence
Featuring elegies on barber boys and pitiful slave girls,
Or free lighthearted advice on the good life.
But I must warn you, throughout this second half
We are going to the gym and the hot baths;
Indeed, we are about to strip; you may not like it,
Suddenly finding yourself surrounded by naked men.
And if some of our dancing-girl friends should pop in,
As they are prone to do, wearing only four roses
And sanitary hair nets (in case we have reclined to dine)
Anything can, as they say, happen.
Mona, you were just putting down my book; you were bored.
Now you won't even look up to listen, you're so absorbed.

The Price

Galla wanted fifty bucks.
I said, "That's far too much."
One year later she asked twenty-five;
"Twenty-five!" I cried.
After six months, she asked again:
"How about twenty?" I offered ten.
A few weeks later she came down to six;
I said I just didn't have it.
Frank paid me the two bucks he owed;
She heard about it and wrote.
It's not a bad price, I replied, but I have debts.
Would she come down to the lowest depths?
She would. She did. She said, "It's free."
But I declined. Galla doesn't interest me.

Someone You Know

I defy you to escape him at the baths.
He'll help you arrange your towels;
While you're combing your hair, scanty as it may be,
He'll remark how much you resemble Achilles;
He'll pour your wine and accept the dregs;
He'll admire your build and spindly legs;
He'll wipe the perspiration from your face,
Until you finally say, "Okay, let's go to my place."

A Discriminating Woman

You sleep with Klaus, with Hans, with Fritz, with Horst,
You sleep with Vanya and Grigori, with Pavel and Boris,
You sleep with Juan, and Pepe, and Poncho, and Tito,
You sleep with Tu Fu, with Wan Tan, and Gung Ho,
You sleep with Paris, with Atlas, with Damon and Pythias,
You sleep with Uncle Tom and the Nigger of the Narcissus,
You sleep with Hymie and Izzy, and Al Raschid,
You sleep with Buffalo Bill and Billy the Kid.
Julietta, you say that you are an Italian woman,
How come, Julietta, you never sleep with Romans?

Diadumenus

Breath of a girl biting an apple,
Aura of early-flowering vines,
Effluence of mountain saffron,
Sweet-smelling sheep-cropped grass,
Myrtle, rubbed amber, Arabic spice,
The fire paled with frankincense,
A chaplet of roses anointed with nard,
Odour of earth in a summer-soaked garden;
Diadumenus, cruel boy, ripe with redolent kisses,
When shall I scent the fragrance of your willingness?

An Epigram from the Portuguese

How do I hate thee? Let me count the ways:
1,206, 1,207, 1,208, . . .

The Sporting Life

He played ball
With a lover's passion.
Now he can't play ball,
He can't play
Anything at all.

Advice to Galla

Galla, how many times will you get burned?
Five or six fairy husbands in a row!
Won't you ever learn
How to say No
To long blond hair and combed-out beards?
These boys can't give you what you need:
And now you take up with sophists.
At least these look like men.
But watch out, you'll get burned again;
Good men are hard.

A Suspicious Distraction

When the wine is poured
By a voluptuous creature
Who easily outshines your wife
And daughter, my mouth waters;
I am naturally distracted
From Indian ivories and new lamps.
Your annoyed glance strengthens my hunch.
If you don't like suspecting me
Of suspecting you, then you must choose
Between luscious servants *and* morals.
Publius, you can't have both at once.

Lines to Charmenion

You are a true Corinthian—
No one denies it, Charmenion.
But don't call me brother.
You skip about with your curly locks;
My hair is stiff and Spanish.
Your cheeks and shanks are smooth;
I've got plenty of rough thatch.
You lisp daintily and inanely;
I've got guts and words to match.
Is a dove an eagle?
Is a doe a lion?
Sister, you're no brother of mine.

Portrait of an Old Pro

Even when you are at home in your cheap flat,
You lie around in an Egyptian wig like Cleopatra,
Flashing false teeth and winking phony eyelashes,
Rummaging through silk dresses in a hundred drawers.
With an artificial face unfit to launch a sinking barge
You expose your manhandled baubles and hoary targe,
Heirlooms borrowed from your great-grandmother.
Still you give out generously to all comers,
And though my battered sceptre is deaf and half-blind,
Your battle-scarred target is easy to find.

This Life

You used to have a bowlegged mutt carry your towels
And a one-eyed monster to guard your clothes at the baths.
A ruptured masseur gave you your rubdown.
How you railed against drinking in those days!
You used to say the cups should all be smashed.

Then your rich old uncle left you his money.
Since then you never go home from the baths sober,
And you have a suite of five pretty boys to help you,
Not to mention the silver embossed chalices they carry.
But you hated this life, when you couldn't afford it.

Choice

A chap who is champ is hard to refuse;
But I like a wrestler who knows how to lose.

Coq au vin

Lewd dinner hosts keep asking you back.
Are you the entrée, or the midnight snack?

Someone's Got to Give

Lesbia says her price is immutable;
But a woman who pays is never inscrutable.

Essence of Thais

Thais reeks the redolence of stale urine
Cracked from an old jug crushed in the street;
The fetid fragrance of a lecherous goat;
The rancid breath of a sick lion;
A dead dog dredged up from the river Tiber;
The unhatched chick of a rotten egg;
An elegant amphora of decayed fish heads.

And in order, cleverly, to hide one odor with another
She parades the bath plastered in green mud
Of shredded peppers and Angora cat dung,
Or pasted in a concoction of chalk and sour wine
Overlaid with three or four coats of jasmine bean flour;
And the essence of all these sticky charades is
That however Thais smells, she smells like Thais.

Not Marble

Dear boy, marble would crush your crescent years
And sink aslant into your Tuscan grave.
Time is as cruel to marble as to tears;
He seizes, unmoved, every prize we have.
Yet Alcimus, accept these gifts I bring,
This grass, these shady vines, this boxwood tree,
And if they die, you know I brought them living
That here shall Honour live perpetually,
Bejewelled with grief and ringed with smiling green,
But nothing heavier than gentle turf
Which bears you back to all you might have been,
The shoots and tendrils of another birth.
Whenever Lachesis spins my life's last thread,
I commend my ashes to such a fertile bed.

"Do You Believe in Fairies?"

Giovanni hurries off to girls,
Gianni wears long golden curls,
Miguel tries to be a he-man,
Manuel cries to be a woman,
Rocco is too fast and greedy,
Paco is too slow and seedy;
But Marco prefers these giddy guys,
Their schemes, their screams, their spiteful lies
To any wealthy marriage prize.

Talent

You have a beautiful voice with true pitch.
You dance gracefully in spite of your limp.
Your history of the Brothers Gracchi is well known.
You are a good grammarian and a splendid astronomer.
Your *tableaux vivants* are always a sensation.

You play the drums,
You play the harp,
You play ball,
You play chess,
You play dead, beautifully.

You swim,
You hurl the discus,
You roll hoops,
You paint,
You sculpt, beautifully, beautifully.

You swallow swords,
You eat live canaries,
You walk on your hands,
You make love in hammocks, beautifully.
The question is—what are you?

"For Envy is a kind of praise."—*John Gay*

I know a guy who's ready to bust
Because I am so widely published,
Because I don't work,
Or clerk, or soda-jerk,
Because I don't teach or preach,
Because I spend my winters at the beach,
Because I keep my summers out of reach
In Barcelona or Ibiza,
Because I sleep with the Queen of Sheba,
Because I live on Riverside Drive,
Because I'm the luckiest man alive,
Because I won't get a Ph.D.
Or catch TB or even VD,
This green-groined bastard hates my guts.
My advice to you is—buster, bust.

A Recognition

You've seen great rumps
On equestrian statues?
Or those large hoops
With tinkling rings attached?
Or a worn-out boot
Full of swamp water?
Or a loose bracelet
That has slipped the claw
Of some consumptive quean?
Or a sagging awning
That won't belly in the wind?
Or a pelican's flabby craw?
That's Lydia!

Getting to Know Laecania

SUD denly she's BRIGHT and BREEZ y
Be CAUSE of ALL THE
BEAU ti ful AND NEW
Denture.

Caveat Emptor

You told me he was an idiot; hence the very high price.
I want my money back; he's rather bright.

Proof

"There are no gods; heaven is empty," cries Segius.
And he proves it. The damned fool thinks he's blessed.

Dining with Zoilus

Have you ever dined with Zoilus?
You could dine more purely with whores.
All swathed in green, he fills his couch alone,
Half-buried in countless silken cushions.
Nearby, his long-haired protégé stands
With a bunch of red feathers to help him belch.
His concubine, on her back, beats with a green fan
To stir a breeze about his monstrous heat.
A small boy chases flies with a myrtle sprig.
My lord is having his daily massage,
Those skilled hands are all over his flabby body.
Now he snaps his fingers; a eunuch responds
And leads him lovingly to the urinal.
He, himself, leans back to the crowd on the floor
Ogling his favorite wrestlers who are gnawing
The tough remains of last night's boar.
Soon we're all drunk on his cheapest wine,
And he's asleep, snoring in our faces rudely;
But we lie about drinking his filthy health.
I don't know why I do it. I really don't!

The Eviction

They're being evicted; here they come:
The redheaded wife with the seven curls, in front,
Then the white-haired mother and the strapping sister.
(Medusa, with Fury and she-bear Callisto).
After them trails the timid husband, chalky and thin,
Nervously tugging at his scrabrous chin;
A three-legged camp bed, a two-legged table,
A lopsided lantern, a bowl with a ladle,
A cracked chamber pot making water through its sides,
A bundle of dirty clothes, unwrapped and untied,
A mouldy brazier, a jug of stinking fish,
Three ropes of garlic and a crawling cheese.
I haven't got a house to lease them;
Neither has anybody else who sees them.

The Father of Seven

Your wife has made you the father of seven.
All too clearly they betray their origin,
The truckle beds and shameless mats of adultery.
This curly-headed Moorish boy is your cook's, easily.
The second, with the flat nose and thick lips,
Is the very image of your brother's bailiff.
The third, with bleary eyes, he's your baker's dough.
The fourth, with queer looks and wide brow,
Ask your aging slave boy if you dare.
And the one with the pointed head and donkey ears,
How could any honest cretin deny him?
The girls—the dark one with the teeth, and the redheaded grin,
A fluter fluted for one, a wrestler wrestled for the other.
You would have more children than Hector's mother,
If your wife were not now attracted to eunuchs.
At least there won't be any more while this keeps up.

The Old Gal

This old gal has three hairs, four teeth,
Cucumber nose, eyes like dried peas,
Complexion of a crab, crocodile jaws,
A hum like a gnat, a frog's voice,
A breath that kills flowers,
She sits at stool for hours
Windy in the morning, gaseous at night.
She has the vision of an owl in the light,
Spider-web dugs, a belly like a sack,
The legs of an ant, a stiff bent back,
She smells like a she-goat, has a duck's ass,
Skinny as a starving hermit at death.
Two hundred husbands she's put under the earth
And now she's rutting to start on her third.
My great-granddaddy called her "grandma";
Who'll want to call this old crone, a spouse?
There isn't a marriage torch under the moon
That could tickle a blaze in this charred ruin.

ARCHERY ACCIDENT: APER'S WIFE TRANSFIXED

When a sportsman weds an heiress
His aim is apt to get careless.

Rialto Exclusive

"My hair is my own." Unquote; Miss Big.
To be more precise—she owns the wig.

Winner by a Yard

At the Athletic Club, whenever you hear cheers,
They're for Big Dick Maron, member without peers.

Wonderful Rome

Rome is wonderful—but don't try to sleep.
Before daybreak, bakers are roaming the streets,
Then the singsong of schoolmasters pedagoguing,
Then the coppersmith's hammer pounding,
Then the moneychanger's coins rattling,
Then the shipwrecked sailor's wooden leg,
Then the boys whose mothers taught them how to beg,
Then knocking; it's a letter, or a book, or a caller;
It's my lady, or my landlord, or my lawyer.
And all night it's drunks drinking, revellers revelling,
Thieves thieving, and soldiers quarrelling,
Litter bearers stumbling, old whores grumbling,
Wives nagging, husbands bragging,
Children yapping, dogs scrapping, lovers grappling;
A murder, a rape, a simple devastating fire,
A bungled suicide, a successful funeral pyre.
It usually sounds as if there has been an eclipse
And everyone is out of doors beating on pans with sticks
To drive away demons. Even up here on the third floor,
The babble of Rome assaults my flimsy door.
Only my country villa escapes this riot.
It's small and run-down, but by Jupiter, it's quiet.